The New World Order

–

Worldwide User's Guide

The Realities of the New World Order

And How They Are Playing All of Us

Against Each Other

Mr. Bob

Copyright 2023 Mr. Bob

All Rights Reserved

Published at Amazon

For my family, friends, country, and world – may we all see the opposing views with respect and courtesy. May we all see how we are more similar than different and realize we are all being played by an evil group determined to divide and control us all. I hope we can unite early enough to prevent the New World Order's plan from being implemented, otherwise we will wind up united to fight to get our freedoms and rights back again after we have lost them.

Table of Contents

Your Author

I think it's important to give you some perspective on who I am and what I believe. I'm sure every reader will agree with me on some points and disagree on some points. This is good. We all have the right to our opinion, to voice our opinion, and hopefully we can have a discussion so we can understand each other. I find that understanding the person I disagree with can be a respectful disagreement.

I have always been more liberal than conservative, but pretty much in the middle. It depended on the topic at hand. On some topics I was more liberal, on others I was more conservative. Everything in moderation as I usually say. I grew up outside New York City, lived there for the first 35 years of my life before moving to middle Tennessee in 2000.

I think there is a huge difference between what is right and what is practical or even possible in terms of legality. I've been saying for many years that I am not a democrat; I am not a republican; I am a realist. I am an independent who votes for who has the better solutions for the most pressing issues at hand. In 2008, the democrat plan to get us out of the recession was better and more practical than the republican plan in my opinion, so I voted democrat. In 2016 I was appalled by democrat politicians selling out our country and their hypocrisy, so the republicans got my vote. At this point I see that most of our politicians on both sides have been bought by the New World Order. We are in serious trouble if we keep letting the New World Order puppet masters manipulate our country's leaders.

I spent 38 years as a firefighter and paramedic in New York and Tennessee. That has made me an outgoing person who can talk to anybody, on the street, in line at the grocery store, anywhere. Throughout my life I have met people from all over the world, in all socio-economic categories from dirt poor to filthy rich, in all colors, all religions, and all lifestyles. I have always found it interesting to learn about people who have a different background or upbringing than I had. I love to hear their perspectives and why they feel the way they feel. I have always been good at seeing an issue from both sides. Even if we agree to disagree, I was able to understand them and can respect their opinion, and in turn, they will hopefully respect mine as well. It is possible for adults to disagree with someone else and still respect them.

Mutual respect and understanding are the first steps in solving any issue we have. That seems to be a lost attribute in the United States and the world in general these days. We have way too many people demanding respect as if it were a right. There is no right to respect. I have found in my career that most of the people demanding respect do not have the character to earn that respect. I give everybody basic human respect to life, safety, and to voice their opinions. After that, respect must be earned, which is not all that hard to do. Show me your character and you'll earn my respect. We don't have to agree, we don't need to even like each other or our respective opinions to earn my respect. If it seems you don't believe what you're saying but are only saying it for followers, likes, and shares on social media, you will not earn my respect. Show me you are genuine in your opinions, truthful in what you say you believe, and can explain why you believe what you believe in a logical manner, and you have earned my respect. Again, I don't need to agree with you or like you to respect you.

A lot of what is going on these days is being intentionally manipulated by the New World Order puppet masters. They are playing all of us to be against each other. I think if we were all to see how we're being manipulated, and instead listen to each other enough to understand each other, we will all find out that we are not that far apart on our views and that we can understand each other enough for a mutual respect and support. The divisiveness in this country is coming from outside sources, playing us all to be against each other. The worst part is, we're all buying into their game.

I'm going to talk about the manipulation of all of us in the next few chapters, talking about the various issues of controversy around the globe. I will be presenting what I have found to be both sides of the issues and giving a few pointers to both sides in how to deal with these issues. I'm sure I'm going to get some backlash for some of these, and you certainly have the right to your opinions. Some people are offended by saying hello to them as you pass on the sidewalk, others are offended if you don't say hello, so I am sure some people will take offense to what I have to say. You can enjoy your right to be offended but take note that I am not trying to offend anyone, just stating facts. Hold your opinions and being offended until the end of each chapter, you may be surprised by the conclusions and advice given.

I'm no expert in politics. These days I wouldn't want to be. I'm just an American who is angered at what the powers that be are doing, how our government is being manipulated by the New World Order puppet masters, and how far this country has fallen in the last three and a half years. I am tired of the back-and-forth banter between both sides, all by planned manipulation. We need to get our acts together and start being a unified country again. We aren't all that far apart if the powers that be would let us have a mature conversation. And that's what they are most afraid of, us seeing through their manipulation and uniting against them. So they keep gaslighting one side to get reactions from the other to play us against each other.

Let's get started with what The New Order is and how they are playing us.

The New World Order

We are all being played by some powerful puppet masters. These people are trying to orchestrate the Great Reset to form the New World Order. Why are they doing this? I have no idea. It'll never be completed in their lifetime.

This New World Order wants a global government under a socialist society. Why socialist? Because the few own it all, that would be them, and the masses own nothing, that would be all of us. What I find confusing is that they are already the richest people in the world, they got that way using capitalism, but they are wanting the world to be socialist. Personally, their money is already buying enough politicians around the world, why not just let it be. Why do we need another world war or worse.

The people orchestrating this New World Order love three-word organizations. We have the World Economic Forum, the World Health Organization, and the various Global Environmental Protection agencies. You know, the people who tell you that you'll own nothing and you'll be happy, the ones who instructed doctors around the world to treat Covid in a manner that caused respiratory failure and death, and the ones who want you to eat bugs while walking, meanwhile they are flying their private jets to meetings to make plans to tell you to get rid of you gas car and get an electric one which is doing more damage to the earth than gas ever did.

I'm not into politics in general, I just hate hypocrites. But these organizations make con men and stereotypical used car salesmen look like they are overflowing with integrity. One of the World Economic Forum's plans is to reduce the world population to 800 million. It is now estimated to be about eight billion people, depending which population count you look at. That basically means 9 in 10 people need to be eliminated. How can they do that quickly? Funny you should ask. Just look around at the world. A pandemic in which the best way to treat patients was dismissed and we treated in a manner that killed many people. They forced a vaccine that produced more adverse side effects and people mysteriously dropping dead than the measly 12 percent effectiveness it was shown to have by their own testing. In the process with lockdowns globally, suicide rose dramatically, as did drug and alcohol addiction. They influenced the younger generations to not want to have children. They also influenced young people that they can't be who they are, so they are mutilating themselves and making it so they can't have children after they've gotten surgeries or drugs that will prohibit reproduction. We have new wars around the Middle East and Ukraine, and terrorism has increased significantly around the world.

Most of us know that money is power. It shouldn't be, but it is. The richest people in the world have been running the world from behind the scenes as long as money existed. This is nothing new. Lobbying politicians, giving jobs to unqualified political family members with the expectation of getting political benefits in return, political donations, and so many other examples exist of how the rich get their way. The recent change is that what was from behind the scenes is now out in the open and obvious to anyone who actually looks at what's going on in the world. The WEF and WHO have announced their plans on several occasions. They've bought the media and the politicians so that if you only watch the lame stream media, you are the least informed of the facts. Folks, we have been brought back in time to 1930's Germany. The false information and propaganda are going full stream ahead in the control of the few who own what you are informed of.

Lately it seems like we are living in either opposite-land or gullible-land. Politicians give legislation a name like "The Inflation Reduction Bill." This was a bill that had absolutely no chance of reducing inflation, but that's what they wanted to call it. We also had the "Border Security Bill" that funneled billions of dollars to Ukraine's border, but none to our own unsecure open door we call our southern border. By doing so, the party that gives the name can say the other party doesn't want to reduce the out-of-control inflation that their own policies induced or doesn't want the border secure. Since the lame stream media won't actually list what's included in the bill, or more to the point won't tell you the namesake of the bill is not included in the bill and that is outright obviously the opposite of what it will produce, we all just keep blindly riding on the turnip truck.

Why are these sorts of things happening? The answer is simple. The powers that be are engineering it to happen. They bought the politicians writing the bill to do what the powers want, they control the narrative, and they control the media. The media doesn't report news now, they inform you of what your reaction should be. Back in the 1990's, we had evening television programs called "The News." They objectively told you what happened that day giving as many details as were available so you can determine your reaction or opinion about what happened. Since the early 2000's, you're told what to think and have to determine if something actually happened, let alone if you would have thought what they want you to think based on what happened. There was saying years ago – "Only the Facts." Now it's "Everything But the Facts."

The New World Order wants us fighting amongst ourselves. United we stand, divided we fall. They are knocking us over. They tell one side what to think and how to react so that the other side will react to that, which they over-emphasize, creating more controversy, confusion, and division. Neither side realizing the initial reports, reactions, secondary reactions, or the reporting of are mostly lies in the first place.

We'll get more into some of those topics as we go, but let's take a minute to look at a plan to destroy a civilization. This could be any civilization, a city, a state, a country, a continent, or the global population. It's not hard to see what the NWO is doing, they are repeating the Nazis in the 1930's. First steps are to control education and start slowly limiting individual rights, starting with the right to free speech by criticizing the government. They bought the media to prevent anything other than their own narrative to be broadcast. They tell you what to think, not what happened so you can decide. They also tell you what your decision should be without any evidence. There are cameras and recording devices everywhere, show me what happened, don't tell me. We play the opposite-land game by the party accusing that the other is a danger to democracy when they are the ones limiting who can run and installing a candidate after the primary election decided who their candidate should be. They are silencing the opposition by taking down opposing posts on social media, making up charges against the key opponent in in the election and allowing extremely biased kangaroo courts handle the sham of a trial. They are also redefining terms that have been used for decades if not centuries to confuse and manipulate people.

Steps after what they are current doing are probably going to be as follows. Limit the population from defending themselves by confiscating firearms. Keep infringing on the rights of the population and eliminating them slowly. Impose fear into the populus to make them dependent on the government. Make it so they must sell what they own just to survive to make them more dependent on the government. An unarmed, dependent population is very easy to manipulate and control. When we get to that, the powers that be will turn on their supporters and we are all screwed.

Looking at other areas of the world we see the progress the NWO has made to make the world a totalitarian police state. What do most police states have in common? They have mass surveillance of their citizens. Look at all the so-called security street cameras we have now-a-days. They have censorship, like when a political party instructs social media to ban posts that conflict their narrative. Censorship is also cancel culture, the media not giving both sides of an issue – only the state's narrative, and the over use of the term 'misinformation' when facts conflict the state's narrative. Police states use ideological indoctrination like what is going on in our schools. Police states will also imprison the opposition voicing religious or political opinions that conflict their narrative. This is what happened slowly over the 1930's in Germany, and this is what we are seeing now in many areas of the world by the NWO puppet masters.

Socialism

Let's talk about socialism for a few minutes. On the surface, it looks benign and fair. It would be great if it worked that way in practice. Socialism is one of the most corruptible forms of society in which a small few people have all the power and the masses have absolutely no power. That power has been abused by the leaders of every country that has gone socialist. It easily degrades into an abusive totalitarian dictatorship. The only way the masses can regain their rights and freedoms is by violent revolution. Which is why the socialist government wants an unarmed population. It's much harder to fight without weapons.

Why use socialism then? Because it is easy to gaslight and virtue signal people into believing socialism would be better than whatever government form is in use at that moment. It sounds much fairer than many other forms of government and is fairer only in the very short term. Then the abuse of power starts and it's all downhill from there. Free stuff sounds great until it's time to pay for all that free stuff through suffocating taxes. Free now but pay triple later – the socialist motto.

I don't think there is a perfect form of government. Power hungry people and greedy people will always try to take advantage of any form of government or society that gets set up. I look for the form of government and society that allows for all its citizens to have the same opportunities to succeed, become rich, and be happy. Looking at the pure forms of government like communism, socialism, fascism, and democracy, none can be successful in their purest form. A combination of forms is needed, one primary form of government with a few programs included to offset some unfair disadvantages to give all people the opportunity to succeed.

There was a college professor that did an experiment. He graded tests as if it was a socialist system with equity – the same results for everybody regardless of the effort put in. Everybody in the class got a B on the first test. The students got who earned an A were given a B for the students who did little or no studying and got a C, D, or F on the test. The second test was graded as a C. The students who were studying realized their efforts were not helping them, so they studied less for the second test. Those who failed the first test but were given a B decided to keep riding the gravy train provided by the students studying. In the end, the students who started out studying a lot and doing well gave up the effort. The students not doing anything liked not having to do anything and getting a benefit to their lack of effort. In the end, the entire class failed the course. That is socialism and equity.

Socialism and democracies are forms of government. Socialism also comprises most of the economic structure of the country as well. Capitalism is an economic structure, not a form of government. Socialist societies generally have started as capitalist socialism before sliding toward communism, eventually getting to authoritarian communism. Socialism is too easy to exploit if you're one of the few powerful people in government. The rest of us pee-ons have no chance of resisting the exploitation even if we wanted to. Want examples? Look at all the countries the U.S. border is being invaded from are coming from. The vast majority are countries that are deep in the slide through socialism to communism, if not there already. If socialism is so good, why are we being invaded by people fleeing socialist countries?

A pure democracy can be just as dangerous as a socialist, communist, or fascist dictatorship. The only difference is how it's done. Imagine the United States in the 1860's. What if the U.S. was a pure democracy instead of a democratic republic. If the popular vote was to keep slavery legal, it would have remained legal instead of being outlawed. We all know that slavery is wrong and unjust, but a lot of people didn't agree with that statement back then. A republic has more checks and balances to offset the latest fads of the time. Any dictatorship or totalitarian government doesn't care what the popular opinion or vote is, they are going to do what they want, which is what is best for them, not what's best for the people.

Nazi Germany in the 1930's began democratic. By the control of the media, taking away people's right to disagree, and disarming the public is what lead to the dictatorship of Adolf Hitler and the rise of the Nazi party. The same methods are being used in the U.S. right now by the New World Order puppet masters. The details are modernized, but the tactics are the same. Look at what other countries that the NWO turned socialist before they targeted the U.S. are going through, my primary examples being Canada and the U.K., but there are many. Those two are starting the slide. Look at Venezuela, Nicaragua, and Cuba for those at the bottom of the slide. I've heard the argument that "they aren't doing socialism right." That is true, but it's the same puppet masters that set up socialism in those other countries that are now concentrating on the U.S. They're going to do the same here that they did everywhere else. That's their plan. They're not trying to perfect socialism; they are trying to be the ones in power.

Socialism is about equity – equal outcome without regard for effort put in. In contrast to that is capitalism – equal opportunities to succeed dependent on the effort put forth. There are no guarantees in life, but capitalism is about anyone that puts in the effort, can succeed. The reality is that not everyone starts at the same point. Support and encouragement from home while growing up, quality education, learning to persevere are not equally attained in everyone's younger years. We have put programs in place to help equalize the opportunities. Finding and taking advantage of those programs is up to the individual. This where that effort begins.

People residing in poorer neighborhoods generally have lower educational quality. Not having the funds to get the best teachers and motivators is a big issue in these neighborhoods. Here's where family influences are most important. Look at Dr. Ben Carson, he grew up poor, his family couldn't help him learn, but they encouraged and supported him to get help when needed, to learn as much as he could, even if they didn't understand what he was learning about. He found opportunities and had the perseverance to become a doctor. He was able to get scholarships and grants for his education and put forth the effort it took to complete his goals. He did it, and so can anyone else.

The last topic I want to bring up in this chapter is how greed plays a role in both socialism and capitalism. Socialist greed is only available to the oligarchs in control. You have nothing, they have it all, and you have no control or opportunity to change that. Capitalist greed is generally a self-correcting issue. If a company or person gets too greedy, there are options available to the public to correct the imbalance. Greed can be good up to a point. It gives people the drive and passion to set and achieve their goals. Greed gets to be a bad thing when it gets out of control. When a company raises prices too high, we have the right and opportunity to buy other products or services. We have laws in place to greatly reduce the possibility of an unregulated monopoly, which socialism does not have. Socialism is a monopoly controlled exclusively by the oligarchs in power.

I've heard the argumentative question asking how much money is enough? In this world we have people too poor to eat well or get medical care, living on the street with no shelter. We also have people traveling on their yachts and private jets, living in mansions bigger than a poor village. Is this fair? There is no easy answer for this. In one respect, who put the effort in to making a product or service to make the money for a luxurious life? In the same respect, who didn't? My opinion – no, it's not fair, but that is life. Many rich people donate money to charities that help poorer people, fund scholarships, and donate in-kind products and services. They also pay taxes to fund programs like welfare and food stamps. There are many opportunities available to poorer people to get them out of that situation, but they have to look for them, accept them, and put them to use. A supportive and encouraging family is probably the most important aspect of success, and that has little to do with being poor or rich.

I said in my "about your author" chapter that I form my opinion about people based on character. As a retired medic, I have met some of the best people in the world and those I don't care for much beyond basic human respect in all categories of wealth, sex, gender, race, and origin. I've met rich people who were generous to charities and gave back to their communities and other rich people I've met who were complete dirt-bags with money (I'm trying to keep this G rated). Some of the absolute best people I have ever met didn't have two nickels to rub together but they were so caring about everyone around them and encouraged everyone they met to be the most of their abilities.

I was never the "star struck" type of person. I can admire someone's talent as a singer, writer, engineer, athlete, or other ability without being in awe around them. I'm more impressed with what they do after the success of their talent. I look at a singer like Taylor Swift, who is a billionaire who made her money singing songs about her bad choices, primarily in men. She is using her fame to promote the NWO agenda by influencing her young fans to vote democrat. I've got a few issues with her. First, as a billionaire, she is promoting the party that wants to "tax the rich." She is the rich. She also knows the rich democrats being elected are not ever going to actually raise taxes on themselves, so she's safe in that respect. If she wants to pay 50 percent in taxes, she can. If not as actual taxes, she could give away 50 percent of what she makes to charities that help the people she is actually taking advantage of. Her music label is currently owned by the same puppet masters of the New World Order who need her influence to further their plan. Personally, I admire her singing voice, but she has done very little to earn any personal respect from me. I see her as a NWO owned and paid for mouthpiece that is detrimental to our society.

I never got the chance to meet one popular person who has earned my highest respect, Kobe Bryant. I don't follow sports much at all, but I know of Kobe. I've heard he was a great basketball player, one of the best if not the best. I can admire his talent but what earned my respect and personal admiration is what he did with his success. He set up basketball camps not just to teach basketball athletic skills. His camps also taught young people about teamwork, dedication, perseverance, and personal skills. The support and encouragement he gave so many young people, many in the absence of getting that at home, is beyond measurement in my opinion. He gave back to people quietly, without trying for political or personal gain, just because he was a great person with the ability to do so. While I'm sure he wasn't a perfect person, nobody is, but his death was a great loss to many.

The Media

Years ago, we had evening shows called the news. They reported what happened over the course of the day. They tried to be complete, covering both sides of an issue, in an objective manner, and left it up to us to decide how we felt about it. Now we're told what to think about something and we have to decide if something actually happened to justify it.

The New World Order puppet masters have bought the news media to make sure we only find out what they want us to know, one sided, overly exaggerated, and mostly made up. When you control the media, you can control the narrative, and control the people.

We have cameras and recording devices everywhere. From security cameras, camcorders, and even cell phones, just about everything that happens gets caught on a camera. Why are people believing the narrative when there is absolutely no evidence to back it up. We all have our knee-jerk reactions to the media's fictitious rambling, which they have designed to keep us from having a conversation to widen the divide. If we got all the information and were able to have a civil discussion, we would all realize that we are all being played and that what we thought we knew was either grossly incomplete or completely made up.

I am a firm believer in the phrase 'Don't tell me, show me." I notice the most important part of the stories I see on the media outlets is missing – the evidence, the show me part. Where's the evidence to show me the story has any credibility. I listened to Kamala Harris, KJP, and the View mouthpieces telling us all how prices were coming down in late 2023 and early 2024. Did you see any prices going down? I sure didn't. The inflation rate dropped a little from the ludicrous rate Biden policies caused earlier in his term, but prices did not go down. Many of you saw the social media post that a guy made showing a grocery order from 2022 consisting of 45 items and a total price of $126.67. He hit the 'reorder all' button to reorder the exact same groceries in 2024. The total is $414.39. The video of him hitting the buttons and showing what was ordered is evidence. All the credible evidence we see is in direct conflict with what we're told. I'll believe what I see rather than what I'm told.

I'll share one more example. Democrat presidential hopeful Dean Phillips was near a Trump rally and decided to see what was going on there. He met and talked to quite a few Trump supporters, informing them of who he was and what he is doing. According to the media, he should have been beaten to a pulp by these violent MAGA Republicans, but he found them all to be "friendly, thoughtful, and hospitable." That is from his post. They actually had conversations like mature adults, not just barking at him like I see in other videos asking liberals about their opinions. We're told one thing, but all evidence is to the contrary of what we've been told.

I would use the media's use of the word 'insurrection' to describe people walking around the capital building but 'mostly peaceful protest' to describe chaos, loss of life, hundreds of injuries, and hundreds of millions of dollars in damages from looting and burning businesses, to be another example of the double standard or opposite-land that I mentioned. That can of worms would fill an encyclopedia size book so I'm going to skip that example.

I use the 'Bob rule' when I hear the media spreading their narrative. The Bob rule is – go two steps further than what they reported. Let's use a media narrative to apply the Bob rule to. Trump is a racist. Show me one thing he did that was racist. His policies helped every American, every American was doing much better personally, professionally, and financially under Trump. I've seen quite a few man-on-the-street videos where people on the street were asked to name one thing Trump did that was against black people. Not one could give an example. We couldn't get one step, let alone two steps to show evidence of the narrative.

Let's do the Bob rule in reverse. Why is the media gaslighting the public to believing Trump is a racist? The NWO, who own the media, cannot buy Trump like they bought the media and many politicians. Trump is pro-America, completely against a global government. And Trump will stand up for what he thinks is right because he doesn't need the job as president, nor is he looking to keep his elected job or to get the next elected job like many politicians are doing. Prior to 2016, he was never referred to as a racist. He was even celebrated for what he did for all people, including all races. But then he went up against the democrats for president. All of a sudden, he's a racist misogynist, without any 'show me' factor to back it up.

I think the media would have been far more successful by reporting what Trump supporters have been saying, which I agree with one hundred percent. Most of us all agree that Trump is an arrogant, pompous jackass. I said it before I voted for him the first time and still agreed with that statement the second time I voted for him. We're not voting for the most popular boy or girl in high school, we are electing the person who is going to run this country and improve the lives of Americans. He did that better than any of these career politicians who promise the world but succeed at nothing. He didn't play politics; he improved our country. As the last holdout of the New World Order, we needed him to not sell the U.S. to them, as the current administration is doing.

Politics and Politicians

The NWO people bought the media to tell you what to think and in turn, how to vote. They want you to vote for the politicians they bought by spreading real misinformation, false narratives, and propaganda through the media they now own. As I see it, the NWO oligarchs bought the entire Democrat party and enough Republicans to eliminate any chance of getting anything done outside of their plan. They left a few unbought republicans so there's some opposition to give the public perception that there is some opposition.

I told you about my – don't tell me, show me ideal as well as the Bob rule. Here's one more – if you talk the talk, walk the walk; if you won't or can't walk the walk, shut up. I usually say that a little stronger, but I am trying very hard to keep this G rated. I hate hypocrites. Take Bernie Sanders for instance, a self-proclaimed socialist. He obviously sees himself as a socialist oligarch because all of us little people in socialism will have nothing and be happy. He's a multi-millionaire with three homes. He talks the talk, but if he wants to walk the walk, he needs to sell his homes, rent an apartment, give away whatever else he has, and live as a socialist. I hope none of you are holding your breath waiting for that to happen. He's one that either needs to walk his talk or shut up, which means he needs to shut up.

I hope the politicians bought by the NWO were promised positions of wealth or power in the socialist society they are working toward. If not, these politicians are dumber than a dump truck full of rocks. They are being bought to sell all of us Americans out. The NWO puppet masters pull the strings, and our politicians do as they are manipulated to do.

It was the politicians that put most of the country on lock down during the Covid plandemic. Yes, I meant it that way. How many politicians were still going to restaurants for private dinners, going to salons, not wearing masks, and going on vacation outside the country. If any of us did that, we would be fined, publicly humiliated, or arrested. Laws for thee but not for me. They knew the plandemic was overexaggerated and the rules were unnecessary, that's why they didn't follow them unless there were cameras around. They kept our businesses closed to the point of bankruptcy, and caused a massive increase in depression, drug use, and suicide. They were basically killing us while telling us they were protecting us. They were just moving as the NWO puppet masters were manipulating them to do.

These are also the ones telling us that walls don't work and that nobody needs a gun for protection while showing us that their homes are protected by walls while they are personally protected by people with guns. Talking the talk but not walking the walk. They really need to shut up. There are far too many examples to put in here, these are just a few.

The last political game I'm going to mention is the blame game. The current administration blames so many adverse effects of the policies they instituted on Trump. If Trump policies were so bad, why did all the adverse effects start after Trump was out of office and the current administration undid the progress he made. The prime example of this is inflation.

Inflation started the second day of the Biden Administration. Biden used an executive order to eliminate the completion of the Keystone XL pipeline. That caused an immediate rise in fuel prices. Every product you purchase gets from where the raw materials are generated to factories for manufacturing, to distribution centers, to stores, and to your home by fuel burning ships, trucks, trains, and cars. Who pays for the cost of shipping the products as well as the manufacturing cost of any product? The consumer. When fuel prices rise because our country is no longer energy efficient, the shipping costs rise, resulting in a rise in the price we pay for the product. This was not just a temporary rise or fall in gas prices, this was a policy of needing to rely on oil originating from other countries, like Russia.

Can anyone tell me why Russia did not invade Ukraine during the Trump Administration? Two reasons – first, Trump is crazy. He gave stern warnings to our enemies not to do anything stupid. The leaders of our adversary countries could not predict if Trump's warnings were credible, but since Trump is crazy enough to be so bold, our adversaries took him seriously. The second reason is that Russia did not have the funds or income to sustain the invasion. That shortfall in funding was resolved by the increased oil production because of the U.S. and several other countries needed to import Russian oil due to Biden eliminating the keystone pipeline and returning the U.S. to energy dependent. Considering the billions of dollars we gave Russia for oil and the billions we sent to help Ukraine, the United States citizens and taxpayers funded both sides of the invasion and war in Ukraine. Congratulations America.

Following the oil induced inflation, Biden policies of spending money we don't have, printing money at will, and giving money to anyone who is not American kept the inflation ball rolling and building like a rolling snowball. But the democrats decided to blame Putin and Trump for the inflation that was well under control during Trump's years in office and didn't start to rise until after Trump was out of office. I was not a fan of President Ronald Reagan, but I agree completely with him when he said the nine most terrifying words are "We're from the government and we're here to help." The democrats need to stop helping us, they're driving us bankrupt.

The First and Second Amendments

The New World Order puppet masters need to keep us divided by conflict. These conflicts are created in general life topics like gun rights, speech, racism, the environment, abortion, gender identity, and anything else they can use to divide us. They use their bought media to distort facts and report only parts of the truth to make as much conflict as they can. By creating conflict in one area, they can expand the conflict with reactions and opinions. The next chapters will all cover how they are doing it for those issues and play the first amendment to maximize the conflict. This is going to cover the process in general terms and then briefly discuss firearms since they are both the only things that are in our bill of rights.

We have the right to express our opinions. That doesn't mean we say anything we want, there is supposed to be an opinion expressed. Yelling "fire!" in a crowded movie theater is not free speech because it creates an unsafe situation if there is not actually a fire. It also does not express an opinion. It may create a lot of the other people's opinion of the yeller being an ass, but that is creating an opinion, not expressing one. The crowd can then exercise their opinions by calling the yeller an ass. Calling the yeller an ass is covered under the first amendment.

All Americans have the right to be offended by another person's speech as well as to offend other people. When two people disagree, both may be offended by the other's opinion. Looking unilaterally that you are offended by ignoring that your opinion offends others is not what the first amendment is about. If anyone is saying things just to be offensive, then they're an ass. If it is your honest opinion, then we can be offended by each other, and we can respectfully agree to disagree.

Cancel culture is the result of people who have no respect for contrary opinions. You will never find me watching CNN or The View because of the absolute crap they spread in my opinion, but to cancel them because I think they're idiots is not what the first amendment is all about. I hope they get taken off the air because enough of the public realize they are mouthpieces for the NWO narrative and go off the air due to lack of viewership. Calling for their cancelation just because I disagree is an immature method of expressing my opinion. They have the right to say and broadcast what they are paid to, I have the right not to watch.

The same holds true for the government pressuring social media companies to limit, ban, or remove posts that go against their agenda. The Biden administration was found guilty of doing just that. The whole point of the first amendment is to make that illegal for the government to do that. If you look at 1930's Germany and the Nazi Party, that is exactly what they were doing.

People post a wide variety of things on social media. They hope to get likes and shares, but publicly posting anything opens you to people and views that disagree. I saw a video posted by a guy in what looked like his early twenties whining about being offended by meat emojis. He not only feels offended by them, but he also says "trillions" of other vegans are as well. That brings up a few questions in my mind to have a conversation with him, like there are only 8 billion people in the world, why can't he remove the meat emojis from his phone if they're that triggering for him, does he know that if you don't look for emojis, you won't find meat emojis, and how 'rich and famous' can he be as a whining entitled jackass that I've never heard of before. He wants meat emojis to be illegal because he's triggered by them. I'm triggered and offended by whining entitled jackasses like him posting stupid videos, can we make him illegal too? We all have the same rights, if we determine that anything that anyone can triggered by should be illegal, life would be illegal.

While I stated my opinion of him, I support his right to post what he thinks. I have the right to form my opinion of him based on his video. I actually hope that was a video just to have something stupid to post about, like so many are, but to just post line after line of meat emojis as a comment to him would be just as stupid as his video. Trolling him just to trigger him shows the commenter is no more mature than the poster. I laugh at videos like that and think he really needs to grow up. I have the right to comment and voice my opinion, but there are times where maturity steps in and I decide not to exercise my right to engage him. Many posts like this go viral because of the number of likes, comments, and shares, so to commenting on it or reposting it as a stupid video just plays the game that he wants people to play.

Let's get into the second amendment for a few minutes. The amendment states that the right to bear arms will not be infringed. What does that realistically mean? There are no limits under the way the constitution is written. However, the U.S. Supreme Court have set some limitations. You need special permits for fully automatic weapons, i.e. machine guns. You can't own an armed an operational fighter jet. You can't own a cannon or cruise missile. What you can own is a rifle or handgun, as many as you want, up to semi-automatic. Semi-automatic means the weapon will chamber the next round, but only fires one round per pull of the trigger. Just because a rifle looks mean does not make it any more dangerous than a nice looking old western rifle.

Most legal gun owners support universal background checks. We want guns in the hands of law-abiding good people. We do not want guns in the hands of criminals, the criminals are the ones we need our guns to protect ourselves and our families from. If the useless, fear mongering, virtue signaling, talking heads we call politicians could write laws that get guns away from criminals, the legal gun owners would support that whole heartedly. The gun laws they are passing or trying to pass only limit legal gun owners, not the criminals. Criminals by nature do not follow the laws. Look at the gun crime in Chicago, a city with some of the strictest gun laws in the country. It's not the legal owners committing armed robbery or murder in Chicago.

Criminals don't fear the police or going to jail, especially in these days of defund the police and release the criminals back onto the street. The only way to reduce crime is to make the criminals fear their intended victim using self-defense.

Now for a few of my personal opinions. I know people who own many guns, all different types and calibers. I look at them and question – how many guns do you need? Now there are guns designed for specific purposes, so someone might want a small game hunting rifle, medium game hunting rifle, big game hunting rifle, shotgun, and a handgun or two for personal protection. While I don't see a need for as many guns as some people have, some people collect guns, and some people just want them. Under the law, they are allowed to own them, and I support them exercising their right to own them. Personally, I don't have enough money for lots of guns. I own a few, based on intended use and which family member would be able to handle the gun. For those who say the second amendment should only pertain to muzzle loaded muskets, the amendment does not state that. That is similar to the first amendment not limiting communication to handwritten letters delivered by Pony Express. The same argument can be made to the technological advancement of the internet. Should the first amendment be limited so it does not apply to the internet for social media posts? Then they apply to the advancements in firearms technology as well.

Since we're discussing amendments, let's take a quick look at the fourteenth. Colorado and Maine were trying to keep Donald Trump off the 2024 ballot by using the fourteenth amendment citing the insurrection farce.

The fourteenth amendment also states that a candidate can be disqualified for aiding our enemies. The Biden Administration policies have aided and enabled some of our enemies like Russia, China, North Korea, Iran, and terror organizations like ISIS to thrive and threaten the United States and our allies. Biden, Harris, and the democrats passing these detrimental policies could have the fourteenth amendment used against them as well. There is also video evidence and proof to the allegations against the democrats. I'm surprised there weren't any republicans trying to use the fourteenth amendment against these democrats as the circus against Trump was in progress.

Systemic Racism

It has been nice to see that people of the general public of all skin colors have recently gotten tired of the media blaming everything that happens on racism. It took till the beginning of 2024 for people to realize it is all a load of crap. Two plus two equals four is racist, being on time for appointments is white supremacy, educational standards are racist, and on and on and on.

That doesn't mean that racism doesn't exist. There are still a few ignorant people out there that are racist and sometimes something happens that was based on race. Blaming everything on race minimized the impact of anything that actually is racist. The word racist lost its meaning and impact. Reality has shown that racist does exist, from all races and toward all races. Treating anyone differently solely because of the color of their skin is racism. Racism is not only discriminating against a race, but also favoring a particular race.

Let's talk about Critical Race Theory. On one side, there is still some racism in this country and world. But should we be teaching children that they are always going to be a victim, they'll never improve their lives, and they will never amount to anything just because they have dark skin? Should we also teach children that they are oppressors, mean unjust people, and they aren't worth being alive because they have light skin. We're not in the early 1800 when those were true. Can we please realize that a great amount of progress has been made to almost eliminate racism until we started teaching children to be racists – white and black. Stop teaching children to hate each other.

What should we be teaching children? We should be teaching children about the heritage and history of all races. We should be showing children that although we all have some minor differences in appearance, history, or opinions, we are far more alike than we are different. We should be teaching all children that they can accomplish anything they want if they put the work in and empower children to follow their dreams. Stop teaching children to be racist and we can stop racism. The more we falsely blame disagreements on race, the more we say math is racist, and the more we play this oppressor and victim mentality, the more racist this country will be.

The media overplayed racism to the point that calling something racist means it isn't. The situations going on in our country that are racist were ignored however or the backward reality game was played. So which side is racist, conservatives or liberals? Let's look at a few examples.

According to the media, conservatives are violent racists. But which side participated in protests that burned buildings, shut down roads, and caused hundreds of millions of dollars in damages? The liberals. How many big protests were there after the 2020 election protesting Biden winning the election? None. And I'm sure the media was looking for anything they could find. Trump is a racist. Why do people believe that? Because the NWO owned media told you many times that he was. Why is it then that when asked for an example to show Trump being racist, no liberal can give one. The reality is that every enhancement Trump policies have made assisted all races, not one was left out and not one was favored. Trump was never referred to as a racist until he was running against democrats. There's a few other topics I'm about to bring up that nobody has an example of the conclusion the media has people believe.

Here's where we going to use the Bob rule. How does two plus two equals four have anything to do with the color of someone's skin or what race they're in? Answer – it has nothing to do with race. Let's go one more step – why would labeling math as racist help the NWO's agenda to get their bought democrats elected? Answer – it is a virtue signaling tactic to divide people and keep victim mentality going, keeping dark skinned Americans voting democrat.

Building a wall is racist according to the bought media. What race is it against? The country is being invaded by illegal immigrants from 160 countries. Which race are we against by trying to stop all these people breaking our laws from illegally invading our country? What do all the democrat (and republican, but they're not playing the race game) protecting their homes with? Walls and fences, that's right. What did they build around the Democrat National Convention in Chicago in August 2024? A wall all around the building. So, walls are racist according to democrats and the democrats are building walls to protect themselves, wouldn't that make the democrats the racists?

Let's talk voter ID for a minute, this is my favorite example of hypocrisy. If you want to say that requiring ID to vote works against poor people who may have a hard time getting an ID, I can see that to some extent. But most states give IDs to poor and disabled people free of charge, and if you can get everything else you need, you can get an ID if it's that important to you.

Someone did a 'man on the street' video asking students at the University of California – Berkley if voter ID was racist. I'm sure they only showed what they wanted in the video, but many white liberals bought into the fallacy and responded that voter IDs were racist. They responded that black people do not know how to get an ID or where to go to get one. The video then cuts to Harlem in New York City asking black Americans if they had an ID and if they thought voter ID was racist. Everyone they asked answered that they do in fact have an ID and they disagreed that requiring voter ID was racist. So white liberals think voter ID is racist against black people, but black people have IDs and don't think it's racist. Other than the NWO bought media narrative, can anyone explain that. Another question to add here – how did they get registered to vote if they didn't have identification?

Let's also ask the important question here. Using the voter ID example, who's the racist? The conservative who sees all voters as equals, who they are assuming already have an ID, who has a job and life that requires an ID to have; or the liberal who thinks that just because of the color of their skin, a black person is too stupid to know where or how to get an ID to vote.

That's a similar situation to all the white liberals who thought the Washington Redskins name was offensive. Before naming the team, the organization asked native American tribes for permission, and they all agreed, saying that they were happy the team will be named after them and were not offended by the name. But the team was renamed anyway for the white liberals interfering in a situation they weren't even a part of. If the native Americans stated the name was offensive, I would support them and their effort to rename the team. But I do not support a bunch of white liberals who have way too much time on their hands with nothing to do. I do not support people who are offended for someone else, especially when the 'someone else'

30

is not offended by whatever the white liberals think might be offensive. And I do not support anyone who is just looking to find something to be offended by, just to have something to do. Get a job, get a life, go out and get (I can't say that), and maybe you'll find some happiness so you don't need to spend all your miserable time finding things to be offended by.

Guess what was needed to get into the Democrat National Convention? A photo ID. Walls are racist and requiring ID is racist. The democrats built walls around their convention and required ID to get in. How racist is that?

Close to racist is slavery. Slavery was abolished in the 1860s in the United States, many generations ago. No American alive today whose family has been in the U.S. for generations has been a slave or owned a slave. Interestingly enough however, Kamala Harris, democrat candidate for President, is not black unless she's pandering to African Americans. Her mother is from India and her father is from Jamaica. Her father owned slaves in Jamaica while she was alive. Also interesting is that Trump's ancestors were never slave owners. Vote for Trump so anyone who has been a slave in their lifetime can get reparations from Kamala Harris and her family.

Global Warming and Climate Change

We've been hearing about global warming for the last 50 plus years. The polar ice caps are melting and most of our land masses will be under water in the next ten years unless we pay more taxes. The same people telling us this are the ones buying ocean front mansions. Why would you buy a home that's going to be under water within a decade. I'd love to hear Barack and Michelle Obama's answer to that from their ocean front Martha's Vineyard home.

Looking at sea level altitudes over the last 50 years we can see the sea is not rising. Plymouth Rock is still visible, and the coast is not under water. What erodes naturally from one area is deposited elsewhere. Polar and glacial ice that falls into the ocean is a natural occurrence that self corrects itself as ice forms in another area. Mortgages are not being denied due to rising sea levels for ocean front property, home insurance policies are not making exclusions so they don't have to pay out if the sea rises and destroys the property. Mortgage and insurance companies would be the first businesses to protect themselves if the sea was actually rising.

Looking at thousands of years of evidence as to what the temperatures were, science has proven the earth has warmer and cooler periods, such as an ice age. The earth's temperature has not changed significantly in the last 100,000 years. Since the earth isn't warming, they changed the fear mongering term from global warming to climate change. Science has proven the climate has been changing. Like I stated above, the earth has been changing for the hundreds of millions of years since it's been here, regardless of how you believe it came to be (Genesis, big bang theory, etc.).

This latest round is about carbon dioxide levels. In the 70's it was the ozone layer, and I've lost track of all the red herrings they've blamed over the years that had no effect on the climate. The earth's climate has been changing continuously for the billions of years it has existed. We had nothing to do with it before humans existed. Are we so arrogant that we think we can destroy the planet short of nuclear war?

I'll bet the earth will recover from nuclear war if it happens. Humans might not survive, but the earth will survive.

The world is filling with carbon dioxide. Scientists have shown that it is currently at one of the lowest levels in history, having been almost eight times what it is now. But it's too high now. And what do the democrats blame it on? Cow farts. And what is the major component of flatulence? Nope, not carbon dioxide, it's methane. What is a source of carbon dioxide? People exhaling, like politicians talking too much but saying nothing, like the ignorant AOC with her New Green Deal and "sees fire," or Word Salad Kamala and her never actually making a point, or Stumbling Joe who can't finish a sentence on the same topic he started it on. If you want to reduce unnecessary carbon dioxide emissions, have them shut up unless they van make an intelligent point.

Time for the Bob rule. Who benefits from reducing or eliminating meat? One of the NWO puppet masters, Bill Gates, is developing meat made of insects, recently getting approval by the FDA. We have had imitation meats made from plant materials for a while now. Follow the money. It leads right back to the NWO leaders. Do you really think he will ever eat his bug meat? Me neither. He'll be eating real steak on his private jet or yacht. We'll be the ones eating bugs while we walk.

The burning of fossil fuels does not release carbon dioxide, it releases carbon monoxide among other chemicals. While cleaner burning engines with cleaner emissions is clearly warranted to reduce air pollution in general, it does nothing for or against carbon dioxide, the substance being blamed for global warming.

What eliminates carbon dioxide from the atmosphere? Plants, grass, trees, flowers, vegetables, and anything growing from the soil. Why should we cut down trees, that take in carbon dioxide and release oxygen that we need to breathe, to put up solar or wind farms to reduce carbon dioxide? Plant life 'breathes' the opposite of animals, that's how the earth corrects itself and keeps itself stable. Plant life is far more efficient and effective at using carbon dioxide than anything else we know of. If this was about carbon dioxide, they would not be advocating cutting trees for ineffective forms of electric production.

Should we do what we can to protect the earth? Of course we should. We should stop dumping garbage in the oceans, recycle and reuse what we can to limit what needs to be put in landfills. We should be doing what we can to limit air pollution by using filters or cleaner sources of energy that are reasonable and sufficient to produce the power needed by society. The most efficient electric power production is nuclear powerplants. There were a few early accidents in the development of nuclear power that scared many to abandon further development here in the United States. Several countries have developed safe nuclear power sources that are very effective.

The plan is for all electric appliances and vehicles to replace anything that uses fossil fuels. Let's use the Bob rule here. Why? Electric items can be connected to internet and therefore manipulated and controlled by outside agencies. I replaced my home water heater last year and it can connect to the home internet. How often do you change the settings on your water heater that you would want it connected to your phone through the internet. I did not connect it; I can walk to it and change it if needed.

The government can shut off your car if you travel too far, they can set your thermostat to an uncomfortable temperature if you set your air conditioner too low for them or heat too high for them, and they can shut down the power grid as they want. Hackers can make chaos if they hack into these systems. In summer 2023 there were announcements in southern California to set their air conditioners to no lower than 78 degrees and not charge electric vehicles because the power grid couldn't handle the demand for electric. Sounds like an all-electric society is not going to work. This is all about control. This is NOT about the planet.

Solar energy sounds great. The sun shines, the panels produce electric. That should help the environment, right? Let's use the Bob rule, one step further. What do solar farms do to the environment that they don't want to tell us. We have to clear the land of all surface brush and trees, we have to dig ditches to run the cable to carry the power produced by the panels, and we need to strengthen the power distribution grid to get the electric produced to where it needs to be. In short, we have to destroy the environment, kill ecosystems of plants, animals, and insects, and use more plastics to make the panels to lower carbon dioxide levels, which the trees we cut down do far more effectively than using electric for everything. In short, they want to have control over you by controlling the electric grid and your appliances and vehicles.

Wind turbines also seem great. Unfortunately, we have to destroy the ecosystems and environment to produce enough wind power as we did with solar. Wind turbines are far less efficient than solar panels, which are not efficient in the first place, so we need more of these contraptions that cost more to manufacture than the revenue from selling the electric power will bring in. It is a losing proposition that significantly increases the cost of electric while destroying the environment. The materials these wind turbines are made of cannot be recycled, so we now have wind turbine boneyards to bury the worn-out blades and shafts. I'm sure the environment appreciates that.

Let's get in to the big one, electric cars. Don't call yourself an environmentalist if you are advocating all cars needing to be electric with the current conditions. There is nothing more damaging to the environment than what it takes to produce and charge all electric cars other than nuclear war.

I'm not against all electric cars. For people who live close enough to where they work and shop to use the electric car as their daily commute and around town vehicle needing to charge the car only once or twice a week is fine. But the range is limited, charging times can be long, the purchase price of the car is high, and the electric needs to come from somewhere, usually coal fired powerplants. If you plan to travel more than the range of the car, it could take your entire vacation just to get there and home again, leaving no time to be just on vacation. My gas-powered vehicle could be fueled in 2 minutes and back on the road, making a 700-mile trip in one day instead of three with a 300-mile range electric car needing to charge twice on the way.

The best vehicles to lower gasoline emissions and use more electric without the drawbacks of all electric vehicles are either fuel cell powered or the new plug-in hybrid cars. You have the range if needed using more gasoline, but the vehicle is charging itself as you drive. If you are in Miami with a 300-mile range all electric car and a hurricane approaching, you can almost make it to Jacksonville if you need to evacuate. The number of all electric cars will far outnumber the useable chargers at any stops you make, creating a shortage of chargers and keeping you in the hurricane's path unless you evacuate days in advance. If this was about the environment and not about control, one of the far more realistic options above would have been chosen, fuel cell or hybrid.

The first issue is mining. The 'environmentalists' are against the mining of coal and natural gas but have no problem with destroying fifty tons of earth to make each battery for a car. Don't say you're against slavery when most of the labor used to mine the lithium and cobalt for the batteries is child slave labor. The damage to the water systems by all the mining, the destruction of plants, animal habitats, and insects is far greater than setting up solar or wind farms.

The second issue is when these batteries catch fire by either exposure to water or thermal runaway. The chemicals released in the smoke of these fires are toxic to anyone or any animal around them. The sheer volume of water needed to extinguish these fires is immense. One large lithium battery fire will wipe out any advantage that another 1000 electric vehicles may have made without catching fire.

The third issue is the production of these batteries and vehicles. The mining of the elements needed are outside the U.S., the cars are being built primarily in China, the batteries are being produced almost entirely in China. Who is getting rich by the production of these vehicles – primarily China. The NWO needs to destroy the economy of the U.S. to succeed, making us dependent on other countries' exports will certainly expedite that process.

The fourth issue is weather. This past winter (2023 into 2024) showed an Achilles heel of electric cars. It was bitter cold in northern states where the cars could not be charged because the battery temperatures were too cold. The power needed to warm the batteries first to be able to charge took almost as long as the charging time. In addition to charging, battery capacity is greatly diminished in cold temperatures, making a 300-mile range at 70 degrees about a 200-mile range at 20 degrees. In those temperatures you will definitely want to turn the heater on in the car, drawing more power from the battery and dropping the effective range to more like 150 miles. Let's add one more complication, a bad traffic accident in the middle of nowhere in an all-electric car with 40 percent charge. If you're stuck on the road for hours, with no way to exit the road, you better hope there's a gas-powered vehicle around with room for a few visitors as you will need to get in with them to stay warm. The gas engine produces enough heat even at idle for the car no need to waste battery charge or burn extra fuel for cabin heat.

The fifth issue is running out of charge. If I run out of gas, I can get a 5-gallon gas can and be back on the road to a gas station in a little while. I love seeing pictures of the all-electric vehicle on the side of the road being charged by a diesel generator, towed by a gas-powered truck. Kind of defeats the purpose of the all-electric vehicle if you ask me.

The sixth issue is range. In addition to the problems batteries have with temperature, try towing with an electric vehicle. Plan charging stops about every 150 miles or less depending on the temperature.

The seventh issue is that lithium batteries cannot be recycled. You want to help the planet by storing these used batteries where they leak chemicals that get into the water supply. That sounds like a troublesome plan to me. The city of Paris France has a grass yard with what looks like hundreds of worn-out electric cars parked. The grass is mostly dead from the chemicals leaking onto the ground.

Last but not least for this discussion is the issue of the electric grid. We do not have a strong enough grid to handle the electricity demand, and we do not produce enough electric power even if the grid could handle it. The vast majority of our power production is still by coal fired powerplants. I've already discussed the inefficient new technologies that are not making much of an impact on the need for coal plants. I've already mentioned California last summer threatening rolling brownouts, so I'm going to leave it with that.

I remember seeing the video of Democrat Senator Debbie Stabenow talking about her drive to Washington from Michigan. She stated she was able to "pass all those gas stations." But what didn't she pass? She didn't pass many hotels with vehicle charging capabilities. The distance from Gladwin MI to Washington is 665 miles. My gasoline vehicle would need one full tank plus about five gallons, a two-minute fuel stop. An electric vehicle with a 300-mile range needs two full charges plus a little. Fast charge stations taking about two hours cost almost as much as I need for a full tank of gas. Or she needs to make this a three-day trip to charge overnight at a hotel. She needed to plan out where charging stations are, that they are not more than 300 miles apart, what the real range is going to be if heat or air conditioning are needed or lights for night driving.

If it was 900 miles and a 300-mile range, unless she started with an absolutely full charge, could get exactly 300 miles per charge, and she could guarantee a charger at exactly 300-mile increments, it would take a third stop to make that 900-mile trip. With gas stations every few miles, I could stop when I want or push the fuel gauge a little lower if I want to. To go from San Francisco to New York City is 2906 miles, 41 hours of driving. A gas vehicle with two or three drivers taking turns driving and sleeping could get there driving straight through in that time. It doesn't matter how many drivers are in the electric vehicle because you need to charge the vehicle. If you couldn't find a fast charger and had to rely on slower charges, that will take you 9 days, even with two or three drivers. The best was Energy Secretary Jennifer Granholm, who had a staffer use a gas vehicle to block the only charger at a Georgia Walmart so the Secretary could use it as soon as she arrived. They held up several other people needing to charge their own vehicles, and got caught for their trouble. The publicity stunt to tout electric vehicles backfired when reality got in the way and a family called the police for this unelected official's manipulation of the system. The new democrat motto: When the narrative you tell doesn't work, cheat, we need the power.

Feminism and Gender Identity

The NWO puppet masters need us divided. They will use manipulation and false information widely dispersed through the media so that nobody knows the facts, and nobody has both sides of any situation. They don't want us being civil to each other, they want us in constant conflict. If they allowed us to talk, we would all realize that we are all being played.

They need to create confusion, controversy, and divisiveness. They change the definition of terms we've been using for decades and centuries to do that. One such term is gender. Gender was generally used as another word for sex. They changed it to an identity term. So, to keep this discussion fair and equal to both sides, I'm going to use the term sex to be DNA based male or female. I'll use gender for the spectrum that is being currently used to describe chosen identity. This will come more into play later in this discussion after we first discuss feminism.

Let get the discussion of feminism started. Feminism started as women are equal to men. Then it went to the second version that women don't need men. Third version was women are men. Finally, we have men are women.

I agree with the first generation, depending on the topic. I think in a relationship and if talking about rights, women and men are equal. That will change depending on the topic though. In general terms, males and females are biologically built for different things. In some topics, men are better at it then women. These topics include activities requiring physical size and strength, long term planning, and logical thinking. For other topics, women outperform men. These include nurturing, math and academics, short term planning, and many others. Men and women are both needed for society to survive and thrive. Men might build the houses, but it's women that make those homes worth living in. And no, I'm not just talking about housework.

Every couple needs to find their individual strengths and weaknesses and divide tasks to maximize the efficiency of the home.

Let's talk traditionally first. The men worked outside the home while the women raised the children and took care of the home. Feminists hate that traditional home style. Women never get a day off, they work from getting up to going to bed, while the men come home and relax. My wife and I have this traditional lifestyle. It works for us and was the best choice for us and our circumstances. I just wish I could just relax when I got home from work. I worked 12-hour shifts, worked through weekends, and had a mentally and physically stressful job. I needed a few minutes on arrival at home to go from work mode to home mode, but then it was fix or maintain the cars, mow the lawn, build furniture, build the shed, fix appliances, and plan how to pay for the things my wife informed me we needed, played with and helped take care of the kids, and help my wife with what she needed me to do. The work done at home was more hers than mine. I have always said and still believe that she worked harder than me, it just didn't generate a paycheck. But the paycheck my job generated was ours. We both worked to support our family.

Could my wife learn how to build a shed, mow the lawn, change the oil in the car, change the brakes, or learn how to do anything that I did? She most definitely could learn and do it all. She just didn't want to. She didn't want to mow the lawn, fix the washing machine, or do most of the home tasks I did. I also had the stress of the family finances, which were tight most of the early years, but I found a way to provide everything we needed and a lot of what she and the children wanted, usually sacrificing things I wanted and cutting back on things I needed.

Does every couple need to have that same system of task division? No, they don't. If my wife was better at fixing cars than me, which I needed to learn how to do, then maybe the laundry would be my task while she took care of the cars. This is where you need to know each other's strengths and weaknesses, so the home runs better, traditionally or non-traditionally. If she had gotten a better job than me, I would be a stay at home parent instead of her. Yes, I would be Mr. Mom if the family would benefit.

Today we have many families in which both parents work outside the home. The division of home tasks would be a lot different in that situation as it should be. These are what need to get worked out by each couple and family. The problem I have with many feminists is that they're not married and have no kids but they're complaining about what successful families are doing.

Women who think they don't need men are just as stupid as men who think they don't need women. Men – your mother who raised you is a woman, your teachers were primarily women, and at some point, the mother of your children will be a woman. Ladies – your father who protected you and your mother is a man, the people who built your house were men, and the father of your children is a man. We need each other.

The third and fourth generations of feminism make no sense to most of us. Women are men and men are women. Sorry, guess again. Can men do most of what women do, yes, they can. Can women do most of what men can do, yes as well. However, look at many of the jobs out there. Men have a physical advantage, so they do more of the physical jobs that the vast majority of women don't want. You don't see many women bricklayers, construction workers, mechanics, and the like. Women tend to be attracted to more nurturing and academic jobs like teachers, administrative assistants, retail, and the like. We generally tend to follow job paths that we would be very good at. I'm glad to see more women firefighters, paramedics, and police officers if they can do the job. I am against physical standards tests that are different for men and women. A fire doesn't burn cooler for women firefighters than they do for men firefighters, the victim isn't lighter just because it's a woman firefighter pulling them out. The job standards should be the same for both sexes.

Then we have the strong independent women. They want to be the CEOs, have law careers, or business executive aspirations. There is absolutely nothing wrong with this. Many want to delay the marriage or at least the children in their lives till an older age. If that's what you want, go ahead and do it. Some women just do not want to get married or have kids. That's your choice and I will support and defend your choice. My only hope for you is that you don't regret your choice in your 50s or 60s like some women do. I hope you are one of the women who are happy with your choice throughout your life.

The same thing goes for men about marriage, family, and career. Same basic choice as the women in the last paragraph, just the male version. My hopes for you are the same as I have for the women.

Now let's move on the dating scene. I love all the video posts of women complaining about men, wanting the 6/6/6 men, or wondering where all the good men are. Too many women are putting all women in a bad light with their posts. They want to be the strong independent woman but wants a man that makes over six figures and pays for everything. Her bills are now his bills even while just dating. It's an insult to her to go to a chain restaurant for a first date. She wants the man to pay for her childcare while on the date or for hair, nails, and makeup for the date. Then they get insulted if he asks what she brings to the table. The honor of your presence is not going to foster a strong relationship.

We also have the women who post that she doesn't need a man and would prefer the bear in the woods. I'm going to guarantee you that if ever encountered a hungry bear while alone in the woods, you're going to be praying that a man, preferably with a gun, hears your screams and comes to your rescue. Men are seeing all these posts that you can do anything a man can do. How are they reacting? They are doing what your posts are asking for. If you can do anything I can do, then do it. I then see a woman's post complaining that several men saw her struggling to carry an air conditioner and they didn't offer to help her. I don't want to say that she personally asked for it, but feminists asked for men to not help, and they are complying. Women are now complaining they got what they asked for.

Men are being told they're not needed or wanted, being given near impossible standards to get a date with a woman, and they're being ridiculed for wanting to get to know her on the first dates before spending large sums of money. Men are tired of the confusion and rejection and they're now preferring the beer over the woman. The good men are staying home or hanging out with the guys instead of dealing with the dating scene. And the beer won't kill him like the bear in the woods would kill her.

Dating is about finding the person whose strengths are your weaknesses and whose weaknesses are your strengths. Someone who has complimentary skills to you and encourages the other to follow their dreams. Not every person of the opposite sex will be a good match for you. Finding that person is the whole point of dating.

What gets me the most are the independent women who bash more traditional women for the choices they made. If you don't want to get married, don't. But don't bash the women who wanted to be married and have kids. If you want to be a single, strong, independent women, go ahead and do it. Most of the backlash you get is from your family. If you're so miserable in life that you need to bash other women, then maybe you should be rethinking the choices you made and deciding what you really want. Feminism should about empowering women. Some are empowered by independence; some are empowered by being a wife and mother. Support and encourage each other. And stop posting negative crap.

Enough about feminism, let's move on to gender identity. One step in the declared plan of the NWO is to reduce the world population to eight hundred million. This means a ninety percent reduction from the current estimated eight billion people roaming this planet. How can they do this? Several ways. They can release a disease among the population with a treatment plan that kills older people instead of curing them. They can also lower the birth rate by making people not want to have kids, or to have people mutilate their bodies to not be able to have children.

The first part of that was started in 2020 by the Chinese, the NWO, and the WHO. The second part is being done by the latest feminism. Put men and women in conflict with each other, not want to be together, get married, or have children. And the third part is through gaslighting young people into believing they are not what they are and chemically or surgically damaging their bodies permanently to not be able to reproduce.

Every person goes through some form of personal exploration in their teen years. You have to figure out who you are, your values, what you like and don't like, and what you want out of life. Everyone goes through this. This is when teens are most vulnerable to gaslighting, especially if the gaslighting seeds were laid in the teen's younger years.

Not every man has to have the physique of Arnold Schwarzenegger or Carl Weathers in the movie Predator to be a man. In the same respect, women do not need the class and femininity of Jaclyn Smith or the appeal of Marilyn Monroe to be a woman. In this I agree that there is a spectrum. Every individual has to figure out their strengths and aspects that make them who they are. No man has every aspect of masculinity just as no woman has every aspect of femininity, not even the ladies and gentlemen I mentioned earlier in this paragraph.

I know several female firefighters that are just as good as any male firefighter out there and can be just as feminine as Jaclyn or Marilyn off duty. You can be a firefighter and a classy lady as well. I love the country Tom-boy cowgirl that can also dress for an event and be the sexiest woman at the event. In the same respect, not every man has to risk his life as a firefighter, police officer, or military member to be masculine. There are many ways to be masculine and feminine without being stereotypical.

I understand that there are people who don't look the way they feel. I'm not going to go through every gender in the modern gender spectrum, but I'm going to divide the LGBTQIA+ spectrum into two categories. One category is LGB, the other is the rest of the spectrum. Here's where I'm going to use the sex versus gender theory I mentioned at the beginning of this chapter. Sex is the binary male and female, based on DNA. Gender is the spectrum of chosen identities. This is to acknowledge both sides of the gender argument fairly.

I am a moderate conservative these days. I believe in the theory - you do you, I'll do me. With the exception of a few ultra-religious people on the right, the vast majority of conservatives generally all think that way. We have many rights in this country, including the right to free speech (expression) and the freedom of religion. While they have the right to believe what they believe, you have the right to not believe that. You have the right to be you.

The vast majority of conservatives don't care what you identify as. We form our opinions of people on their character, not their identity. Will I say that male women are female? No, I will not. However, I do respect their right to be themselves, I will defend their right to be themselves, and it does not affect my opinion of them. Character is what I find most important. The issue that's happening lately is that people in the TQIA+ community think and announce their identity as if that's important. It may be to you, but not to conservatives. Why is it that the LGB community doesn't have similar problems to the TQIA+ community? Because they show their character without announcing their identity or pronouns.

I have heard that many of in the LGB community want out of the LGBTQIA+ spectrum. I understand that. Hearing LGB people talk, theirs is a preference of who they find attractive. It is not an identity issue. A gay man knows he's male, identifies as a man, just prefers to be with another man. A lesbian woman knows the same, just in female form. Bi-sexual people identify as the sex they are and are attracted to people of both sexes. There's also the latest conflict in the alphabet community where trans-lesbians are calling lesbians transphobic because they don't want to be with a trans-woman. Let's keep this in the realm of reality. A lesbian is homosexual, not homo-gender-ual. They don't want a person with a penis, regardless of what they identify as. LGB people are binary people who do not have gender dysphoria. Someone will have to explain to me how a person with a penis, even one who identifies as a lesbian woman, who wants to put her penis in a female's vagina, is not actually a straight male-man who likes to wear dresses. If a trans-lesbian identifies as homosexual, they should want to be with another trans-lesbian, of the same sex and identity.

A lot of the conflict between the SLGB (straight, lesbian, gay, and bi) communities and the TQIA+ communities is self-acceptance. I am who I am. I'm nowhere near perfect, but I accept who I am, as do the vast majority of the SLGB people. We live our lives, we go home to who we go to, we don't have to wave flags to let everyone know what we are, and since we accept who we are, we don't need anyone else's acceptance, validation, or approval. We don't force our lifestyle on others, we don't need to announce our genders or pronouns, and we don't demand respect or validation.

I have friends. I have friends that are straight, friends that are gay, friends that are lesbian, friends that are bi, and while we're on the subject, my friends also include people from all races and many nationalities. I can't say I know many trans, queer, non-binary, or other people in the rest of the alphabet community, but I have met several. One in particular, who is most memorable, was a patient I had. I was assigned to a pedestrian struck by a car. I arrived to find a woman on the street dressed in a nice sexy but modest dress, who was hit by a car and had some pain from it. Part of the assessment for injuries included checking the integrity of bones. As I assessed her, I found something I was not expecting. I don't think she realized I saw it at first, and luckily, I was experienced enough to not stop the assessment and continued on. The situation didn't get awkward until we were leaving the scene to take her to the hospital, and she apologized to me for not telling me she was male before I found out. I reassured her it was not a problem. Luckily, she was bruised a bit, but nothing obviously broken. We had a great conversation after that. I think she didn't have anyone to talk to, and I am a great listener, so she opened up to me. She told me she has always been more comfortable with herself living as a woman. She was open, honest and genuine. She impressed me with her character, so I have no problem using the pronouns 'she' or 'her' for her. I am forever grateful to her for allowing me to get to know and understand her. We only had a short time to talk, which was interrupted by medical questions and activities, but I got to understand her quite a bit.

She is what I refer to as truly-trans. On the flip side are the trendy-trans. What is a trendy-trans? It's a person who chooses to be trans for likes, shares, or attention. They post videos and pictures just to create or inflate conflict, or just to get likes and shares, but aren't who or what they claim to be. They are jumping on the gender identity band wagon for personal gain. They keep raising the bar on ridiculous new identities and pronouns. If I was a truly-trans, I would want the trendy-trans to stop. The trendy-trans grossly and negatively impact how the truly-trans people are viewed by non-trans people. These are the ones demanding respect without showing any or earning any. They are the ones causing the most conflict with threats. I love the latest new gender, the semi-bisexual. They are bisexual but only prefer one sex. That makes you straight if you prefer the opposite sex as you, or gay or lesbian if you prefer the same sex. Bisexual means you prefer both sexes, hence the 'bi' which means two, and 'sexual' meaning sex. It's not a hard concept. In short, they are just playing a game at the expense of people who are genuine in their identity.

The leading two in the trendy-trans category are Dylan Mulvaney and Lia Thomas. We start with a fifth rate actor who couldn't get a role if his life depended on it and who prostitutes probably raised their prices for when they saw him coming. Not making it in acting, he decided to play "first day as a woman" to get likes, comments, and shares. He is doing this for the publicity, and the controversy just adds to it. I will give credit where credit is due, he can play the likes and shares game. He has played the game so well Bud Light made him their spokesperson, costing them millions in sales and stock price decay. But Dylan made a lifetime worth of money. Now he's a lesbian, he wants the opportunity to put his penis in a vagina. The good news for him is that there are women out there that will have sex with him to ride the publicity wave. To us reasonably thinking people, he's a straight guy who needed a ploy to get laid.

Then we have the two hundred forty something rated swimmer. He realized he couldn't win against other men, so he decided to compete against and beat women instead. And the feminists support this. If the feminists think they can do anything a man can do, then why aren't the women athletes beating the male athletes? I'm all for empowering women, but males have an unfair biological advantage over women in physical competitions. We'll get back to this at the end of the chapter.

The same goes for the queer, nonbinary, multiple gender, and the rest of the alphabet spectrum. I can't keep up with all the new pronouns that I'm supposed to guess and use. They want mandatory use of their chosen pronouns. Now, are there people who are trying figure out who they are and don't know how to describe how they feel? There sure are. These are the equivalent of the truly-trans. Most of these truly people will eventually figure themselves out. Until then, it's hard to understand how someone is a man, a woman, and nonbinary all at the same time. That's both sides of the binary coin and nonbinary. That's physically impossible. The trendies of these genders seem to make new crap up as they go. Now we have people identifying as seasons of the year and using pickle pronouns. Do you really wonder why we are all getting tired of this? The more they make up, the harder they push for acceptance. The harder they push, the more pushback they get, and then they whine about it. Quit forcing your dysphoria on everyone else. Be yourself, quietly. You can't force respect, you can't force acceptance, and you don't act in a manner that will earn either of those.

The next problem the trendies cause is from their refusal to converse. Ask a trendy to explain what they feel, and they'll bark, scream, call you transphobic, etc., anything but answer. Why can't they answer? I don't know, they won't answer that question either. If you want people to respect and accept you and your identity, you need to let them understand you. Take the question "What is a woman?" I'm not asking to trigger anyone, but there should be an answer other than "anyone that identifies as a woman." If there is no definition to what a woman is, then how do you know you are one? That makes you a widget – an imaginary object. The long-standing answer has been that a woman is an adult human female. The trans community would object to that, and I understand that. But how about an answer like a person who exhibits mostly feminine traits and qualities. That answer is at least a real answer. Not everybody will agree with that as being a complete answer to what a woman is, but I can respect that answer. Giving an answer like that shows some character as well. It opens a mature conversation that we can build on. But that's not what the puppet masters want.

Someone who was gaslit will give the 'anyone who identifies as a woman' answer. They're only told what to think, not why or how. They can't explain anything, even how they feel or why they identify as they do. They give the best evidence to the gaslighting theory with their circular answer or the ones barking. They don't have an answer, they can't have a conversation, they just want to make noise.

Let's take a minute to talk about those who identify as other species. If you want me to accept that you are a wolf, walk the walk - live in the woods, kill your food without weapons, and sleep in a cave. If you're only talking the talk, but eating with a fork and knife, sleeping in a bed in a home, and shopping at the grocery store to come home and cook dinner, I'm not buying it. I have a few questions for the parents who believe their children are cats. There's a few videos of people upset that a school doesn't know how to handle their cat child. I see the responses from opponents to the identifying as a cat, but I haven't seen anyone ask the most obvious question. Why are you sending a cat to school? If you are the parent of a child who identifies as a cat, and you truly believe your child is a cat, then why are you sending a cat to school. Cats don't go to school. That should be the first question. In my opinion, these parents are gaslighting their kids in their attempt to make noise as a trendy.

I try to be as accepting as I can. But there are some situations that just go beyond my tolerance for noise making. There was a trendy-trans woman stuck in an elevator. He used the call button to get help. The front desk clerk answered, and since the trans-woman has a deep voice called him sir. The front desk clerk was just trying to be polite. The trans-woman told the clerk that he'd rather be stuck in the elevator and called ma'am than out of the elevator being called sir. Years ago, if I was the clerk, I would have apologized and gotten the person help. Nowadays with the trendies just looking to make noise, I'd answer by telling him: "That's fine ma'am, call me back when you want us to get you out." So many others just look staged or scripted.

Just a short talk on the gender pay gap. First off, the liberals complaining about the gap are assuming the gender of the statistics based on sex. If you get offended being misgendered, then don't do it to others. Second, the statistics took the gross income of males and females to compare. It did not take into account the number of hours worked, which is higher for men. If a man and a woman work the same job for the same hourly rate, but the woman works an average of 46 hours a week while the man works his 40 hours, she will have a higher annual salary. It doesn't account for dangerous jobs that are primarily done by men and therefore pay better. Why don't you see women working at a construction site? A woman is more than capable of operating a bulldozer or excavator, but the few women I have ever seen at a construction site are directing traffic. Traffic duty doesn't pay as well as a heavy equipment operator.

Last thing for this chapter, I promise, is sex and gender in sports. How do we make it fair for women in sports? If we're going to allow male trans-women to compete against female women, we might as well just have non-sex or non-gender sports. It's just a swim meet or soccer game, no sex separation, everyone competes against everyone else. Another idea going around is to make a separate category for trans-people. I could go for that, although the logistics needed for a third category will probably be a problem for the sports promoters. Lastly, we can change the name of the categories from men's and women's to male and female, or XX and XY categories. We definitely need to do something. I'm sure eventually even the feminists are going to realize that they're not empowering women by having them get beat by men.

My advice to everyone, regardless of your sex or gender, is to figure out who you are without interference from others, accept and respect yourself first, and stop looking for others to accept or validate you for who you are. Stop listening to the gaslighting, it is only making your journey to figuring yourself out harder. Some people won't accept you no matter who you are or what you identify as. That's life. You don't need anyone to accept, respect, agree with, validate, or approve of you. Let other people know your character instead of announcing your identity or pronouns. Live your life and allow others to live theirs.

Election 2024 and the Future

There's a lot riding on the election in 2024.

We have the incumbent democrats telling us they are going to fix the economy that just three months ago were telling us how strong the economy is. They've been announcing for years how great Bidenomics is working. That's why the 2024 Walmart re-order mentioned in the fourth chapter, The Media, is three and a half times what it was in 2021. That's why most young people need to live with their parents due rent prices that skyrocketed under Bidenomics. If they're policies were as great as they've been gaslighting us to believe, then why do the same people who made those policies so great need to fix them, on day one as Word Salad Harris claims.

Bidenomics is the initial economic effects of socialism. You will own nothing and be happy. If that were true, why aren't most liberals happy? You own nothing, can't afford rent or food, you should be the happiest people in the country at the moment. You've got what you voted for. You should be celebrating and enjoying your victory, socialism is upon us.

Biden, Harris and the democrat party have done more damage in three and a half years than any other period in history. We are dealing with several wars going on in the world that all have the potential of expanding to another world war. But on day one Kamala Harris is going to fix all the problems she helped cause.

Look at how you personally were functioning four years ago. Could you afford to eat? Could you afford rent? Could you afford to do most of the things you wanted to? You might not have liked the so-called mean tweets because they were factual. You might not like the president on a personal level, but was he running the country better than how it is now? You're not going to agree with everything he did or everything he wanted to do, but we're not electing the most popular person in high school, we're electing a president to run this country. Do you want the country run better than it is now, or do you want it run into the ground, the direction we are currently heading?

Do you want your U.S. taxpayer money staying here to help the U.S. population or going overseas to other countries? Do you, as a citizen or legal resident, want to see your taxpayer money paying for rent and food for military aged men who invaded this country illegally when you can't afford what we are providing to them for free? Look at what the democrats are wasting your money on and decide if that's okay for you. Oregon is starting a program to give $25,000 to help illegal immigrants buy a house. If you're a U.S. citizen, you are on your own. How long do you think we can sustain that? I have no problem helping other people who need help, but only after we are taking care of our own people. Also ask yourself this question – Could you use that help instead of giving it to criminals? If that answer is yes, then vote republican.

Let's talk reproductive rights for a moment. Roe vs. Wade being overturned did not make abortion illegal. It was overturned by the U.S. Supreme Court only because abortion was not mentioned in the U.S. Constitution as a right. There are plenty of things in the country that are legal but not listed as rights in the Constitution. Driving laws are authorized in all 50 states and not listed as a right in the Constitution. The U.S. Supreme Court's decision made abortion laws a state issue, not federal. The right to bear arms, the right to free speech, the right to religious freedom, and many others are specifically listed in the Constitution.

Before the Supreme Court's decision, most conservatives were against abortion, but also had compassion for women who find themselves in a situation that is detrimental to their future. Before the Supreme Court's decision, abortions were generally allowed in the first trimester. As the liberals stated - safe, legal, and rare. I'm not a fan of abortion. I hope nobody out there is getting pregnant just to get abortions. That's not good for anyone's body. I do understand how an unexpected pregnancy can adversely affect a woman's future though and when safe, legal, and rare, can be determined to be a woman's better choice. Where did this get so out of control? When a state like California tried to make abortion legal up to 28 days after the baby is born, and other states making abortions legal up to the minute of birth. If you can kill a one-month-old baby, you are a special kind of evil. I'm still trying to figure out how a woman can carry a baby to full term and decide to terminate it as she's in labor. I'm sorry, but at that point, that 'clump of cells' is a baby. Calling a fetus a parasite and several other absolutely ridiculous statements from the left caused an equally as ridiculous knee-jerk reaction from the right to ban abortions. If we all compromise a little, keep it safe, legal, and rare, we can find a compromise and pass laws that are tolerable by all. The NWO puppet masters want us being so extreme that we will never agree or compromise. Both sides fell for the NWO's game on this and many other topics in politics.

Conservatives have challenged liberals looking to make this country socialist to live in a socialist country for six months to see what it really means. I don't think that's a bad idea. They're not saying the 'love it or leave it,' they're not telling you to move out, they're just saying that before you advocate for socialism, maybe you should experience it first hand for a while to get an up-close and personal taste of what you're voting for. See up close and personal how miserable life is under socialism. If socialism is so great, why are most of the illegal aliens invading this country fleeing socialist countries?

The pro-socialists have responded with a challenge for conservatives to live with a minimum wage job for six months. Well, I have news for you, we did. For years I made minimum wage in my early to mid-20's. I made $3.35 an hour. How did we do it? We worked overtime (72 hours a week while also in college full time), we shared expenses (split a 2-bedroom apartment), limited the latte factor expenses, we fixed what broke instead of replacing, and we bought used instead of new. We made it work. We did have one major advantage though. We didn't have Bidenomics causing skyrocketing inflation, we had lower taxes due to not giving taxpayer money to everyone except Americans.

Minimum wage jobs were never designed to be family supporting jobs. Put in some work, get experience, and move up in position and salary. If you want better than minimum wage jobs, you need to develop or learn better than minimum wage skills. I put in the work, got higher certifications, got longevity raises, and got the experience to get a better job with better pay so I could afford a family. We all did it back then. Nobody starts as the CEO unless you started your own business, which is also an option. This is nothing new other than now we have young people wanting the rewards that we older and experienced people have worked for, without doing any of the things we did to improve our financial situation. You can eat today if you're handed a fish. But if you get a fishing pole and learn how to use it, you'll eat for life without needing someone to hand you a fish. Again, put in the work, get the rewards.

If you're going to go to college and can't pay cash for it, study in a major that leads to a job and career. Basket weaving, gender studies, and any of the vague majors I see students in that don't lead to a career are a waste of your time and money. I paid for my college, had taken some loans and paid them off. Also take a math class so you can learn that if you have $70,000 in college loan debt and pay only the interest plus $12 principal a month, you will take 52 years to pay it off and it cost you ten times the initial amount in interest. Big banks make most of their money from interest. Credit cards and loans being the primary means for interest. There are plenty of websites and apps out there that will show you how long it will take to pay off and the total interest paid for any loan. Most bank websites have these loan calculators. You might need to start at the minimum payments but pay more as you can to get out of that debt faster and pay far less interest. I shouldn't have to pay for your useless degree, or even a useful degree. If your degree doesn't lead to a job or career, you shouldn't have incurred that debt. If your degree does lead to a career, then you shouldn't have a problem paying back the investment you made in yourself. My taxes and donations help fund scholarships, put the work to get one of those, that I support.

When choosing who to vote for in 2014, think about the following:

Do you like the financial situation you're in now? Do you want to lose what you currently have? Do want to own nothing and hope you might be happy? Do you want a female president whether she's qualified or not just to have a female president? Do you not want to own a home? Do you want to not be able to feed yourself or your family? Do you want to help everyone else, including criminals, despite the hardships you are going through now? Do you want war and terrorism to be everyday fears in your life? Do you want to lose all the rights you currently have? Do you like getting word salads and dances instead of answers to America's problems? Do you want to be completely dependent on the government for everyday survival? Do you want to be under totalitarian rule? Do you want a government that is a mere puppet of a global plot for a single world government (the NWO)? If you answered yes to every one of those questions, vote democrat.

The democrats like to call conservatives Nazis. But look at which party is doing what the Nazis did in the 1930s. You might not be noticing the censorship yet because you disagree with what is being censored. Look at the party that is trying to disarm citizens who legally own firearms. Look at the party who is pushing for socialism. By the way, the Nazis convinced the population all the changes being made were for the greater good, as the democrats are doing right now. Once they got in power, nothing that they promised came to be. If you're in the LGBTQIA+ community – name a totalitarian government that allows any of those lifestyles. They are all illegal. If you're also pro-Palestine, they want you dead. You're against a conservative who thinks a person with a penis is a man, but you will support a group of people who will kill you in a heartbeat just for being LGBTQIA+. Think about that. Use the Bob rule, show me the evidence. I can show you videos of what Muslim extremists do to the LGBTQIA+ community. They really taped their torture and murder. They are not for the faint of heart, they are bloody and sickening to watch.

If you want to afford to live a reasonably comfortable life, if you want the rights you have, if you want to have the opportunity to put the work in to improve your life, if you want to live in a free society, if you want afford rent or buy a house, if you want to afford to eat, if you want peace in the world, if you want the best person as president regardless of their sex/gender/race, if you to keep what you have and expand on that, if you want to help Americans first – then others as we can, if you want answers to issues, if you want a vote in what happens, and if you want to be free of totalitarian rule, then vote republican. At least for this election.

I told you before that I am not a fan of Donald Trump as a person. He can be an arrogant pompous jackass at times. But again, we're not electing the most popular person in high school. The president of the United States should be putting America first, that's their job. He did a better job than Biden and the democrats over the last three and a half years.

If you are better off now than you were four years ago, you are one of the very few lucky ones. If you were a teenager during the Trump years, do some research, look at inflation rates, affordable housing, and the ability to exercise your rights. Ask for the evidence to back up what you are being fed by the lame stream media, you will find they are feeding you nothing but lies. Just because you heard it on the lame stream media or internet doesn't mean it is true. Use the Bob rule – go one or two steps further, asking who profits or benefits from you thinking the way they want you to think and what thinking like that does for them. Follow the money.

Parting thoughts:

Don't buy into the lame stream media. If you're being told what to think about something, look for the evidence. If they can only tell you, and not show you what happened with a little before and a little after, so you have the context, they are gaslighting you. When they tell you to "look at all the great things this administration has done," try to find some specific things that are better. If they are not naming any specifics to back up their statement, that's gaslighting. Show me, don't just tell me. If there's no evidence to back up their conclusion, it's a fabricated story to gaslight you.

Use the Bob rules. I just mentioned the show me rule. But use the one or two steps further. Why are they telling you what they're telling you? What do you have to gain by it? Probably nothing, except being their misinformed puppet. What do they have to gain by it, either in money or some form of power? What is their benefit to you believing what they're wanting you to believe.

If you really think socialism is right for this country, do your own research. Look at what happened in other countries that went socialist, like most central and south American countries like Venezuela or Nicaragua. If you're in the LGBTIA+ community, look at how they used that same community in that country and notice that being in that community is illegal in just about every totalitarian socialist country.

Look at the plan that the New World Order has announced. Do you think they are genuine in their goals? I hope you see through their puppet mastery. They will be flying their private jets, eating real meat, and doing anything they want while you are regulated out of having anything or being happy.

We are all being played. Stop falling for it and start fighting against it. If this country continues to fall apart like the last three and a half years, you are going to hope we southern conservatives hid some of our guns from being confiscated and decide to fight for you.